Present

Present

by

Amy Lai

Inkstone Books

PRESENT
© 2004 Amy Lai, all rights reserved
ISBN 962-86740-2-1

Typeset in Centaur by Alan Sargent
Printed by Lightning Source in the US and UK

First printing 2004

This book is sold subject to the condition that it shall not, by way of trade or otherwise, be lent, resold, hired out or otherwise circulated without the publisher's prior written consent in any form of binding or cover other than that in which it is published and without a similar condition including this condition being imposed on the subsequent purchaser.

Inkstone Books (a division of Chameleon Press) http://inkstone.chameleonpress.com
23rd Floor, 245–251 Hennessy Road, Hong Kong

Contents

Preface 9
Acknowledgements 11

Storybook

Once Upon a Time 14
Garden Corner 15
Black Sheep 16
The Panda Rubber 17
My Tabby Cat 19
The Picture Book 20
Big Sister is Watching 22
Hello Kitty 24
Duckling Gaze 25
Happy Ever After 26
Little Red Shoes 28
As the Clock Bangs 29

Swording

Pivot 32
Revenge 33
Metapoem 34
Peeping 35
Dumping 36
Set to Baffle 37
World Teacher, *To John Dent-Young* 39
Try Hard 40
Through Time Tunnel 41
They Write, I Write 43
Black and White 45
Surrender 46

Cambridge

Night Plane 50
Introduce Myself 51
At the Picture House 53
A Room of My Own 55
Grannies 57
Holiday 59
Night Calls 60
Food Allergy/Allegory 61
Filming Fleeting 63
Midsummer Common 64
Apology to Bing Xin 65
Leaving 67

Rhapsodies

Intertextual 70
She Flees to Him 71
Ask 72
Burial 74
Borderline 76
I Caught a White Kitten 77
I Returned a White Kitten 78
Roses 79
Morning News 80
Kleptomania 81
Before Night Meets Dawn 82
Bluebird 84

Contents

Present

    Kind Man Pious Woman 86
    Performativity 87
    $20 88
    Unplug 90
    Cup Noodles 92
    Screens 94
    IOU 96
    Mother's Choice 98
    MTR 100
    Love in the time of SARS 101
    Do I Dare? 102
    Birthday Present 103

    About the Author 105

Preface

To WITNESS the successes of students and former students is one of the greatest pleasures that teachers can experience. Readers may imagine my joy, when I heard some years ago that Amy Lai had impressed the external examiner of her M.Phil. dissertation and then that she had gained a place at Clare College, Cambridge, to read for a doctorate in Literature. I was even more pleased to learn some three years later that she had obtained that doctorate from what is still one of the greatest universities in the world. To write a preface to Dr Lai's first book of original verse in English, her second language, is a double happiness, because I write not only as a teacher but also as one poet celebrating the first book of another poet — one who lives in a part of the world we both know and which has been an inspiration to us both in our different ways — Hong Kong.

The sixty or so poems printed here have been arranged into sections but all deal in one way or another with the quest for self and a grasp of reality amid that music of youth, that is always a perception of what Amy Lai aptly calls the 'sonata of uncertainty' — see her poem 'Before Night Meets Dawn'. Does this mean that Lai's verse is musical? Not entirely so. She uses mainly the vague 'free verse' lines favoured by numerous writers of twentieth century verse, usually living in North America. She follows the colloquial rhythms of English, sometimes even slangy English, in the midst of standard usage. Her verses are grouped either in irregular verse paragraphs or in stanzas of four or more lines. In a few poems she uses rhyme, either *abab* quatrains or couplets. She is preoccupied in some poems (e.g. 'Mother's Choice') with trying out some of the musical effects of English as well as working with

Preface

her good girl/bad girl themes, yet she is also searching for her own particular *voice*. When she writes in English, as here, her voice seeks expression of the Hong Kong-British hybridities seen through Chinese eyes and as experienced by her modern Hong Kong sensibility.

This collection, Lai's first book of poems, contains work already seen in literary journals in England, as well as other poems, printed here for the first time. It gives us snapshots of perception relating to childhood and schooldays in Hong Kong, life at the Chinese University, and a more independent, if lonelier, adulthood as a Cambridge graduate student. Among her explorations are multicultural experiences, the search for a room of one's own, love and sexuality, painful transitions into adulthood, internal conflicts, self-doubt, and the Cambridge milieu. This is a young woman's book but it is not just a book for young women. Some of it is journalistic — reportage — like 'Love in the time of SARS' but the depth of feeling we expect in a true poet can be tested if we dive into 'Happy Ever After' or consider the biting ironies of 'Little Red Shoes'. A charm and sincerity comes boldly to the fore in 'World Teacher', her homage to one of her best teachers, the translator and poet, John Dent-Young.

What is promising in Amy Lai's work, what suggests she will continue to write and publish? I think one can find that promise in her, if one looks at 'Try Hard'. This is her first book but it will not be her last.

ANDREW PARKIN

Acknowledgements

THE YEAR 2003 was a turbulent but rewarding time in my life. Armed with a graduate degree in literature, I entered a related field, Cultural Studies, with its vibrant world not only of books, but also of cinema, television, cartoons and fashion. The cultural critic, a new role on which I have prided myself and which earned me new experiences of study and immersion in various cultural texts, has also enriched my life and my creative writing.

Looking back, I deem it a blessing to have met the people who suspended their disbelief in the ability of a new scholar like myself, and who helped to pave the way for my fantastic experience. I must thank Prof. Angelina Yee and my other colleagues in the Division of Humanities at Hong Kong University of Science and Technology. My destiny also put me in touch with Prof. Wimal Dissanayake again, whom I had met briefly, years ago, as a master's student, and who was trusting enough to offer me the opportunity to explore the world of cinema and write my first academic monograph on a Hong Kong film.

By dramatising the year 2003, however, I am tempted to forget the other marvels and sweet surprises in my life. I first read Prof. Agnes Lam's poetry a few years ago, and her work evoked homesickness in me when I was still caught in the midst of writing my dissertation in England. She is now a colleague and fellow writer — albeit in another university — and I count it my luck to have known her. She was willing to dedicate much time for commenting on my original manuscript, and she inspired me to revise it and write new work for the final book.

Acknowledgements

Indeed, ever since I came back to Hong Kong, I have continued to receive support from the good people I have known for a long time. They include Prof. Tam Kwok-kan, my former teacher at the Chinese University of Hong Kong, and Prof. Andrew Parkin, another former teacher of mine, who took the trouble to go over the manuscript and write the preface for this book.

It is a wonder how much pleasure writing has always brought to me. I started writing in my early teens, with the encouragement of my loving parents. Whether with the pen or the keyboard, it enables me to resurrect cherished memories from the past and re-live them all over, crossing boundaries of time and place and making the *present* — the here and now — even more intense and worth living.

This book is my *present* to all the people who love me, and all the people I love.

AMY LAI
DECEMBER 2003

Storybook

Once Upon a Time

It was one October afternoon.
The sky was an azure dome
and the air smelt of lemonade:

One October afternoon
I was done with the last class,
expected a bottle of Vitasoy at Franklin
and a visit to Swindon;
perhaps a tour of Shatin Plaza
followed by a sweet nap:

One of those afternoons
I almost heard music
and saw lovely people walking
across the green with streaks of light
hanging on their hair and
gathering into pools of gold
on the grass:

One golden afternoon
my eyes still lingered on things
and they gazed at a shining figure
till he was translucent with light
and I caught a pair of wings
on his back:

Wink —
I drop out of the gold,
fall in my chair,
click the keyboard,
snap the picture closed.

Garden Corner

Eyes closed,
she now retires
in the cool of the bush:
her ears trembling to
water trickling;

Hush —
the cat is tired,
having fed her
five newborns.

Black Sheep

The sky was blue,
the sun was red.
Brown hills, yellow soil.
On the green, green grass
white lambs looked like
cotton-clouds in the sky.

Dad rushed out to work
while mum started the chores.
The teacher stepped in
and students bowed.
The lesson began
and we must listen:

Look — this is a deer;
that one is a horse.
Now repeat after me:
Dee-eer — dee-eer — horrrse — horrrse —
No, this is a horrrse
and that is a dee-eer!

Left alone that night
on a white cardboard,
I rubbed the sky red, the sun black;
a green grimacing moon —
my own shadow towering
over the fiery soil.

The Panda Rubber

'How are you, m'dear?'
Her mum asked
helping her off the school bus.

'The pencil case was there,'
she sobbed, 'but the panda rubber
disappeared!'

'So you got back the pencil box
you left in the drawer yesterday?'
So soft was mum's voice.

'The girl who shares my desk
in the A.M. class —
she must have stolen it!'

'The one you met the other day
at the stationery store?
The storeowner's daughter?'

'That was the last one they had!'
she choked, 'It was so cute!
I won't find another one!'

'Maybe the panda was too cute —
she took it home, and will
return it tomorrow.'

'Maybe it was lost —
she dropped it as she opened
your pencil box.'

'Maybe she was greedy —
her parents do not
teach her to behave.'

'Or maybe her parents —
do not buy her gifts,
nor spare her stationery.'

My Tabby Cat

No soft, furry darling
you'll find at Sanrio or Toys"R"Us —
a resident of Chung Kiu,
her eyes twinkled with solemnity;
her matted skin shone like
the silk lining of padded Chinese jackets;
and her odour carried the aroma
of classical Peking furniture.

'Papa, let me hold your hand!'
I fitted my little hand inside my father's palm —
heart fluttering — feet pulling to the window —
hand squeezing an extra dose of sweetness
into hand.

She meowed, somersaulting with me
on the soft blankets and
lost her lustre as years shed away
further lost her voice
after many a tumble wash
till Chung Kiu was gone
after two decades tumbled topsy-turvy —

Then I remembered her,
my eyes watching TV news in the red hot summer of 2003,
mind chasing the past from the present and
churning the past with the present
clutching the past in nowhere.

The Picture Book

'Go do your homework,' sis chided,
'Throw away nonsense stuff!
This is out of your syllabus!'
I dismissed her, gazed at *Snow White* —
I found my face in
her fair skin, her black hair;
my red lips pressed with desires,
my eyes narrowed with visions.

'Come join us to *yum-cha*,'
dad barked as usual.
Caught in the middle of *Little Red Shoes* —
I jumped off the chair, stamped my feet
and shot him an angry glance.
I smeared lip-colour with trembling hands,
dabbed blush over unpowdered skin
and tore my body from the mirror.

'Bedtime,' mum said, 'Now go to sleep!'
I looked up from *Little Blue Beard* —
my face flushed, my head sweating
all with fear, yet with greater anticipation.
'If you don't go to bed, darling'
she warned me as I hugged the book,
'I will go into such a terrible rage that
it's better that you do!'

'Open me! Open me!'
I heeded the tempting voice,
tiptoed out of bed, fumbled for the key,
unlocked the drawer, took him out,
looked around, turned over his cover —
an uproar penetrated the room,
gathered into a plunge and
swept me off my feet.

Big Sister is Watching

I tiptoed along the chilly corridor
and jumped
as the mouth of the elevator opened
and she appeared.

'Hey — you!'
The floor trembled
beneath my feet.
'Hey —'

I turned around,
walked to her,
heart thumping,
back straight.

Didn't the Commandments read:
Thou shalt not wear long hair.
Thou shalt not wear accessories.
Thou shalt not wear makeup.

'Good Morning,'
she said with a smile,
faint and meaningful.
I re-gathered my self,
nodded and murmured:
'Good Morning Sister.'

Thou shalt respect your teachers.

I slipped down the stairs
and felt my face burn:
it must have been so flushed —

I licked those glossed lips,
which she didn't notice,
making them more shiny.

Hello Kitty

Kitty, Kitty,
you got no mouth?
Can you speak, kiss and eat?
Shhh! It's here —
under my fur.

Kitty, Kitty,
why hide your mouth?
Why whisper, not talk?
My man will look for it
and love me more.

Kitty, Kitty,
whom do you kiss?
Your sis, teddy, or your man?
I play with bear bear
and dream of Daniel.

Kitty, Kitty,
aren't you hungry?
You want some fish?
Nah, nah, I must slim up —
light me a joss stick.

Duckling Gaze

'The ugly duckling is condemned and isolated,
but it grows up to be a beautiful swan
and is worshipped by all,'
Hans Christian Andersen tells us.

Hence my secondary school teacher
doted on a cute classmate and announced to the whole class:
'I remembered her since Day One —
I found her very pretty.'

But on the topic of 'Keep fit' another day,
she teased a fat classmate who happened to walk past her desk:
'So you wanna keep fit?'
She could not hide her amazement, learning that
she was a choir member —
it certainly takes a 'fit' girl to sing well.

On the MTR my friends told me:
'She likes you too, 'cos you are smart
and so *duckyee*.'
Yet I did not know
if her gaze was one
of contempt, or concern;
nor was I certain
if ducklings can indeed
turn into swans —

not until I pictured the small thing,
listened to its quacks, looked into those eyes
to realise there is neither cruelty, nor irony
in Andersen's tale.

Happy Ever After

Once upon a time my pals flicked their tongues
over coffee cups: 'With his looks and background
you could expect him to be cool and snobby',
while I sat and brooded on his nods and smiles.

Well-read in Andersen and Brothers Grimm
they told me that I was a 'plain Jane',
a Cinderella-wannabe at my best.
'He recognises you? Impossible!'

I gazed into my cup, turned it into a cauldron,
chanted in silence and conjured the meetings;
Slowly images gathered, spiralled and rose —
I saw those haunting eyes again, and smiled.

But a decent girl must not embarrass herself:
I sent my blessings, shied away,
stole a last glimpse of his back —
and joined my pals for more coffee.

For all their wicked characters
fairytales do not reach the human jungle,
where paints hide beneath paints on hunters' faces
and painted faces confuse hunters with the hunted;

Neither do they spell out 'attraction',
which does not forewarn its prey;
abrupt, intense and fleeting:
it needs no rationale, be it coming or going.

Silence makes the heart grow fonder —
but to him I must issue this 'thank-you' —
a visitor from a brave new world,
who urged me to live my own story.

Little Red Shoes

I caught a pair of shoes
as I waited for the school bus
in front of the boutique.

'They're too mature for you.
When you get older — older,' Mum promised.

After a shit week at office
I decided to pamper myself and
traded my pay cheque for

the new red shoes and danced
to myself lightly and steadily and
danced back the child in me

but my feet were sound and
I realised there ain't no punishment
as there ain't no need at all.

'You are just every other
Hong Kong woman —
superficial and greedy!'

I'm a woman, ain't I?
'How old are you, woman?'
'She's old — No bid!'

As the Clock Bangs

I watched the girl; I watched her skipping rope.
The girl was me: on my face was not a line —
I told myself, and yes, I felt the hope:
Her smiles reflected my smiles; her eyes were mine.

And here you came, hugging a Monchhichi.
'It's round-eyed like you, and it sucks its thumb!'
But then I couldn't bear such love for me:
Still smiling, in my throat I felt a lump.

The girl still skipping, the seconds slipping.
I bade you stand with me before the mirror —
The clock started banging, the girl stopped skipping —
I avoided your face, which must freeze in horror —

I'm sorry, we've reached the end of the book.
Oh why, do you now give me such a look?
As if I haven't forewarned you all along!
I slapped it shut, with fingers crooked and long.

Swording

Pivot

'Women who become writers,'
claims Erica Jong,
'very often do so
to gain a rank in
the male-dominated world.'

But I sword my way,
locate the pivot point
where pen meets paper,
only to expect the
'click' of bodies.

Revenge

That burning day
You caught me off guard
First flamed my wound
Then burnt my grudge.

On the same night
I held my weapon
Found the right spots
Plunged. Twisted. Split.

The slaughter done
I did not bother
To clean my hand
With Persian water.

One bright morning
I found your blood
Jet black and square
As prints on paper.

I sharpen, re-sharpen
Certify deaths
Dig epigraphs on
Coffins. Urns. Graves.

Metapoem

A lady, thighs closed, sat beneath the tree.
'Those were the days when sorrows were at bay —
In shades, on benches, hand-in-hand,' wrote she.
'We smiled and laughed and cheered and cried *hurray*.'

Her thoughts were running — Chinese words she played:
'Then came the days when we're plagued with sorrow —
You sighed in chapel, while I soothed and prayed,'
She went on, 'for a better tomorrow.'

Amazed, and thrilled by the power of words,
She poured, 'At last the moment must arrive —
The day we parted, we thought things couldn't get worse:
We spared our tears and farewells: well, that's life.'

This Chinese poem did earn her Third Prize.
A sixteen-year-old, learnin' to try her luck —
I wrote to win; hence I dared not cry 'Yuck!'
I knew my thoughts — true thoughts — would soon arise.

Peeping

With keen interest —
he walked up
and down the narrow aisle,
lingered at my desk,
and moved and lingered:
peeping at my work;

Secretly flattered —
I caught him peeping,
my right hand raced down the squares
and my left hand re-adjusted the book
so that the examiner
could read better.

Dumping

Nights turned heavy
since I stopped writing,
brooded in the dark,
laden with thoughts;

but the paper tempted
with all her whiteness
before I steamed,
tore her to shreds

and stuffed the body
into a new vase:
a slender witness
blooming fresh pink —

I turned away,
but my eyes caught
her swollen body:
throbbing transparent.

Set to Baffle

'The girl,' I said,
'sets her heart on the school
after she missed out the chance of
meeting with the guy she fancies,
who is a graduate there.
Yet by the time she arrives,
he is nowhere to be found.'
And the story ended here,
beautifully, lyrically.

'But the story is incomplete!
It's certainly missing something,'
complained a reader.
'Isn't it built on the same old plot:
meeting, separation, quest
and reunion, so typical of
young-generation writers?
Only it leaves out the last part,'
a critic remarked.

Then I confirmed, as some said,
that women writers are readily
misread by males,
intertextualised and blinded
by their own prejudices
to the richness of language;
and by female readers,
who cannot live beyond romances,
nor transcend their personal spheres.

Reluctant to get didactic, I replied,
'The story has to end at that point,'
though I expected no approval,
only funnier questions:
'Will there be a sequel?'
'Is it autobiographical?'
I suppressed a giggle, knowing
the girl has now grown up —
a woman, determined to baffle.

World Teacher,
To John Dent-Young

My writing course tutor
with his Cambridge accent
conjured an England
in the mind of an eighteen-year-old:

A red-roofed house with snow-dimmed windows
that expose fragments of a wintry garden;
the family chatting over British tea
and homemade buns on floral-patterned dishes;
grandchildren running a toy-train in front of the hissing fire
and his silver-haired wife tugging the yarn from a lazy kitten —
next to him in an old armchair —
dozing to the sweet tune of the piano....

One day my coursemate
told me about his Chinese wife
walking next to him at New Asia College;
later I found his translation (with his son)
of *The Water Margin*
and learnt of his tours and lectures
in Sri Lanka, Spain, Burma and Thailand.

To him who has travelled half the world
and now back at home,
I write this poem with regret
for being too shy to pay my visit;
I pen the last lines with double gratitude
for his kind words a decade ago.

Try Hard

I thought I made
my heroine unique:
her life no mimicry,
her passion no quotation,
her opinions her own.

But she turned to me,
laughing derisively,
'Moral or immoral,
your story is anything
but well written.'

Through Time Tunnel

Time seemed to linger
in my supervisor's room
in that old college building.
I checked my watch —
even the clock seemed to lag behind.
'Or does it?' he asked.

'I haven't got an email address,'
he said, and in case my letters
took a whole day to get to him
I played the postman, walked
all the way to Pembroke and
left messages in his pigeon-hole.

The pendulum swung as
he frowned and went through
the thing I last sent him.
'Wrong expression —
nothing is "very unique" —
either it is, or not.'

'Don't drag the sentences:
cut them short, split them in two,'
impatient again.
'And beware of redundancy —
no "the" before Hong Kong society
as this cannot be more definite.'

And briskly he drew the conclusion
in the same way as he did before,
hitting the nail on the head:
'Don't assume the reader knows.
If you want to say something,
spell it out; make a statement.'

Relieved that the meeting was over,
I walked down the wooden stairs
that spiralled and squeaked,
re-entered the sunlight,
feeling reborn, curt, precise,
Upbeat.

They Write, I Write

Those are the 'talented ladies':
they use their studio pictures to grace book covers
illustrate their works and publicise on the Net.

Apples of students and OLs and housewives and lonesome men;
experts in love and romance and everyday matters and every
    single matter;
spokes-ladies of the love-struck love-sick love-less young
    generations:
to fulfil their missions and reward their fans
they meet you at the annual book fair —

There! There!
Their close-ups are shot,
their looks are rated,
their fashions are price-tagged,
the queues at their counters, gauged and compared.

'It's hard to be a writer nowadays!'
a commentator shakes his head.
'No, it's damn easy to be one,'
replies a cynic.
'But it's a glamorous career!'
another envies.
'Well, I'm just an ordinary person,'
says a modest talented lady.

I read and listen,
not without amusement
like I did the recent years:
my eyebrows raised at the
Hong Kong Chinese writers of popular romance fiction,
my spectacles dropped,
as my fingers keep stringing more a-l-p-h-a-b-e-t-s
into w-o-r-d-s into
i-m-a-g-e-s.

Black and White

My body becomes
Font 12 letters:
Sooty between fingers;

But the name resurrects:
Black ink on white silk,
Starchy and steamy.

Eat! I shout. *Eat!*
I choke their groans
With Hard Facts.

Surrender

Sorry, but Wordsworth sounds lame —
'powerful feelings' are more than
a 'spontaneous overflow',
and emotions are hardly recollected
in a tranquil state of mind.

This would sound schizoid
to psychiatrists and the like,
but how often can feelings
be put down, yet not put down
one way or another?

Biding farewell to the Romantic,
I turned to the Expressionist,
but found it overbearing;
the Cubist, more flat than cubical;
the Abstract, utterly abstract.

Shall I chart the magically real
out of my mental labyrinth,
gathering history with folklore,
merging fantasy with reality
and mixing nominal with verbal?

Or shall I turn to the Avant-garde,
repeat scenarios in slow motion,
conjure thrown-away images,
and paste signs and symbols
in out-of-tune colours?

My pen ceases being a sword;
monstrous signs now scutter
across my computer screen —
like that of a newborn kitten —
my mouth opens, but utters no sound.

Cambridge

Night Plane

Strapped in my seat
I was tempted to get up,
but the seat belt
bounced back on me,
whilst the air current was
rocking the plane.

Somewhere above Central Asia
I restlessly repeated to myself:
I was on the right plane
because of the invitation
in my backpack;
because of mixed expressions
on my parents' faces;
because I was flying
to my dream place;
because someone had teased me
for daydreaming:
'Join the summer school instead —
it's not the place for you.'

Introduce Myself

1998 —
Things were getting worse
but my hallmate blurted,
'Hong Kong! Wow!
Some interesting things
are going on there!'

My supervisor asked me
the first time we met:
'Are you from China?'
'Erh — I'm from Hong Kong.'
'Well, but Hong Kong
is part of China now.'

A new friend guessed:
'Are you Chinese?'
'Yeah I am!' —
so happy that I'd never been
mistaken for Japanese
like my fellows were.

'But you don't look like
Japanese at all,'
another friend told me.
Sure — so proud I am
of our own heritage:
our culture, looks, air.

Xu Zhimo —
the bard who introduced
Cambridge to China —
Now I wonder why
I never shared
his works with them.

At the Picture House

Some say Cambridge is a white place,
where coloured faces are still rare —
in classrooms they huddle in small groups,
and when Gao Xingjian won the Nobel Prize
few voices spoke —
such monotony and inertia,
even our college chaplain
frowned.

On St Andrew's Street cars roar past the cafe
where people chat and eat and smoke round small tables;

At the Picture House upstairs,
the audience dives through Screen One,
through the canvas of Peter Greenaway's *Pillow Book*
into the flesh, colours and calligraphies
in a vibrant world of French, Chinese, Japanese;

A white tourist stops an Asian guy, mutters, and
walks away and lingers on the street turned flashy with lights;

In front of Screen Three,
I peep at the sordid world of *Intimacy*,
abhorred by its flesh and messiness,
but soon sweating with Claire and Jay
in a London basement;

An Asian student babbles about the greasy food,
crossing the street on his way back to Emmanuel College;

Screen Two at the centre,
the biggest of all,
is crammed with an audience
too eager to ride the *Crouching Tiger*,
fly over rooftops, fight in the bamboo forest and
wander across the Gobi:
here is an audience
who sighs at Li Mu Bai's death speech
(at which the average Hongkonger
bursts into laughter),
sheds a tear or two at hearing
'A faithful heart makes wishes come true',
and starts a debate on the meaning of the last scene
and Jen's destiny as the curtain draws;

While the street roars on as the audience descends the stairs
and pushes open the door and joins the roaring in the street.

A Room of My Own

Here porters with bowler hats
greet you at the lodges,
canteens serve fish 'n' chips,
and people crowd in the MCRs
to watch the BBC.

I hurried across
the British Old Court,
ran over Clare Bridge,
climbed up the stairs
to my room at Thirkill.

On my ancient desk,
Xu Xi and Agnes Lam
welcomed me back
to a small Hong Kong:
textual, but real.

We overlooked our
Southeast Asian neighbours:
Catherine Lim, Simon Tay,
Shirley Lim and others
on the table nearby.

This was a hybrid space:
times and places collapsed
in Timothy Mo's Canton,
London and Hong Kong,
re-mapped on a shelf —

Images kept flashing
on the computer screen,
juggling for space
in this room of my own,
that was no room.

Grannies

They say the Brits are racists,
and beware of old women —
frowning and pigeon-eyed,
mouthfuls of complaints.

On Sydney Street
an old lady walked past,
clutching her umbrella
in the British way,
then turned round
to flash her smiles at me,
whilst our eyes lingered on the doggy
that stood between us —
wagging its tail.

At the toyshop
a granny cuddled a teddy
and chuckled to me:
'It's so cute, isn't it?'

I was resting my head
on the table at Woolworths:
an old woman sat down,
touched me lightly on the arm
and handed me a cup of lemonade.

I would have suspected
a stranger's motives,
had I been in Hong Kong.
'Are you feeling better?
Do you want some food?'
I shook my head and
fumbled for my wallet,
but she smiled: 'No dear!
Someone would have done
the same for you.'

And she left me
a sunshine of smiles
a granny would leave
her granddaughter.

Holiday

A month ago
Mum frowned at my luggage:
of *Thorntons* chocolates
Beatrix Potter animals
Monsoon fashion —
my desperate attempt to
carry place with me.

A month later
I stuffed an extra suitcase:
ginseng tea and scallops
birds' nests and CDs —
homing a campus
defamiliarised,
once again foreign.

Night Calls

11pm.
I woke up to the ring,
jumped off the bed,
picked up the receiver,
groaned *I am fine*,
then ran a hot bath —
while waiting —
checked my email.

(Note: Oh Agnes, I was not jetlagged.
I often felt so tired after walking back to my room that I fell into bed immediately, waking up only at the call from my parents. . . .)

Food Allergy/Allegory

My Indian hallmate at St Regis
next to her loaded fridge
offered to spare me
a dish of hot dinner:
she tended the fire, checked her watch,
her hubby was coming home —

But I said 'bye-bye' to her
and her spiceful kitchen:
red, green, gold, black....
spared myself the allergy
and dined on sliced salmon
bought earlier at Sainsbury's —

Raw flesh down the throat,
flesh slipping down flesh
massaged the mind and soul
with the deep sea smell.
Running and pulling,
my thoughts gathered momentum —

Chocolates itched my face
and I did fine without them.
Yet, yet, once in a while,
like when new brands arrived
or simply the heart was lured
by the rush of chemicals —

Expectant and child-like,
I travelled all the way
to Harrods in London
like there was no other day.
The mind — a child's or a woman's —
isn't that hard to fathom.

Filming Fleeting

Leaving the library, I walked along a path of sunlit petals while wrapping myself up with the scarf and pulling the sleeves of the floral sweater, newly bought at Monsoon, down my palms. It was not long before I saw a tall blond greeting me from afar and asked myself who it was. Yet he already walked by and as I turned round to catch him he waved me a good-bye, leaving me still baffled as to when and where I met him. I recalled the same thing happening some months back outside the gate of Memorial Court and I was just as forgetful. My memory took me further back to a year ago outside the Old Court, when my face must have betrayed me to the effect that the woman, who turned out to be a college staff, reminded me of her name straight away —

I turned right to Kings Parade and my eyes were greeted by a montage of the gothic and the modern, village green and running traffic. Such elusiveness typical of my home city had been carried abroad to a new place for three years, and it now confronted me as strongly as ever with a fleeting train of human faces. In this place that I was leaving, my heart yearned to hold on, and my eyes had struggled to film the disappearing — as if I had tried to catch the flowers in April and was left with fragrance on my sweater.

Midsummer Common

At dusk I sat alone on the green,
drowsing, trying out
the proper channel to tune in.
The Shakespeare Festival
had died down,
though characters in period costumes
still fluttered in my mind —

    I rose after sunset,
but in that blue moment
before darkness descended,
my eyes detected something
at the tree bottom,
among the mushrooms,
tiny and moving —

    I am still wondering
if those were mental images
of *A Midsummer Night's Dream,*
or indeed the faeries
the child in me
had longed to see
that last summer in England.

Apology to Bing Xin

'I never waste a piece of paper
but have always kept each sheet,'
wrote the young Bing Xin,
'so that I can fold
many a little boat,
lean out of the ship
and release them one by one
onto the river.'

But how can a child
relate to 'Little Boat: To Mother',
her renowned and most recited poem?
Why no letter? And why paper boats,
save her poetic license to impress?

It failed on me, but
I did share her literary interest
and her life path of
crossing the sea:
she went to Wellesley
and I went to Cambridge.

Walking back to my rented room one tiring day
I heard punters bemoan the end of season,
while the wind from the North Sea
gathered and whispered.

I glimpsed back at the river
that wound nowhere —

for the first time
her poem rang
a chord in me.

Leaving

I last saw a Cambridge night
when it wasn't quite night yet,
but darkness had descended
as the cab took me from
St Regis to the terminal.

'I will charge you less
since I took a wrong turn,'
apologised the driver,
as the lights before my eyes
coalesced into a yellow blur.

'So cold,'
she took out my luggage,
'You know,
there was snow last night.'
I nodded. I had not slept.

It was a freezing evening
in early November.
I inhaled an early winter —
my fourth winter there —
my farewell gift.

Rhapsodies

Intertextual

The air smelt masculine.
She wallowed in the daze of
his sun-soaked features,
as he flipped the papers with hands
that would guide the untrained body,
murmured *great* and *excellent*
in an ecstasy of approval.

Turning against the heat
to catch the last trace of odour,
she dived into his sea of works,
weaved sentence by sentence,
erased entry and exit:
she locked him gently —
too gently to notice.

She Flees to Him

It's menopause in twenties: life sucks her dry:
But sitting face to face with you-know-who
Chases back days, months, years, and returns the 'I'.
'That's all? Got more questions to ask, have you?'

One more second — it won't cost you a dime!
Oh God, have mercy: I do nothing wrong!
I just pray that you will spare me more time:
Not greed or lust — just my wish to stay long.

'Don't tell me you were out for no reason!
Answer! Where the hell have you been these days?
Ask yourself what you have done since Day One!
Repent, confess, then return to your place!'

Enough! I stomp, seize, slap away the bore:
Return is out of question — I rush ahead.
Night falls, and I reach his place, face all red:
I know he will smile, softly, like before.

Ask

'A faithful heart
makes wishes come true,'
the saying chimes
in ears of the suffering.
Have faith, and you'll be saved.
'Ask, and ye shall receive.'

Hypnotised by the magic of words,
trying to imitate art with life,
she went to Wong Tai Sin
and squeezed into sweaty crowds.
She mingled with housewives and nannies
and rotated windwheels with them.

She bought crystals of all sizes:
rose red, purple, yellow and black.
She used her hands to feel their vibrations.
She convinced herself they trembled.
She studied and revised the testimonies.
She counted on them for changes.

At Trevi Fountain in Rome
she tossed her coins and prayed.
She called upon the Roman Gods
for the energies of holy water.
She prayed that next time she was there
she wouldn't be alone.

Back in the chapel she brooded
like she had as a child.
She recited 'Our Father' — 'Hail Mary'
and whispered her sorrows.
She pained and numbed her knees
and felt her face wet with tears.

'Ask, and ye shall receive.'
A closure, much less a goodbye,
if anything, if anything —
would restore her peace of mind.
Isn't that good enough
in an era as such?

Burial

If someone tells me that he loves me, I wouldn't be thrilled — unless his love can be cashed. By the same token, I wouldn't worry if someone told me that he hated me. Look. Doesn't the sun rise as usual? And don't the flowers blossom as before? Fuck! Those who hate me might well eat their hearts out. Who cares?

    Yi Shu, *Hei Bao*

1.

last word uttered
door clicks
footsteps fading —

    sobs

2.

i wrench it out
(painful, yet bearable)
wrap it
in a velvet cloth
(it's still warm)
put it
in a padded box
(it throbs all the while)

lock it
into a
safe
(doesn't it shriek as the key turns)

where the heart is
and will be

key dangling
i stride down
the echoing
corridor

painless
sobless

hollowed

Borderline

Smoke and drink
till the body rots —
don't you know
being 'good'
won't bring any good.

Slash the wrist
till the pain explodes —
like they say:
an aura of fragility
will turn any man on.

I Caught a White Kitten

The fox gazed at the little prince, for a long time.
'Please — tame me!' he said.

'I want to, very much,' the little prince replied.
'But I have not much time.'

        ANTOINE DE SAINT-EXUPÉRY, *The Little Prince*

The other night
I caught a white kitten
shuddering by the road.
So I picked her up,
caressed warmth into her body,
carried her to the lawn nearby,
spared her a piece of raw fish
from my sushi box —

    then I left the thing,
pulled up my collar
and walked away.

I Returned a White Kitten

'It is your own fault,' said the little prince. 'I never wished you any sort of harm; but you wanted me to tame you.'

'Yes that is so', said the fox.

>   Antoine de Saint-Exupéry, *The Little Prince*

Before I left
I returned the kitten to you
'Are you sure you won't miss her?'
Tickling her head
you looked into her eyes
for your own image.

'Nah,
but it'll be difficult for her —
not 'cos of me though —
cats, unlike dogs,
are attached to places,
not people.'

Roses

The red, red knots
cover the back and
blossom into a garden,
dragging the soul with
the weight of eternity.

Hence I hold my breath
as the blade falls,
till the redder emerges,
burning petals with leaves
and pain cancels out pain.

Morning News

The rising steam dispersed
and revealed the close-up
of a disowned woman
before she jumped off the roof.

In its aftermath,
I took the egg out the boiler
and witnessed the shell crack,
revealing a claw:

I wrapped my palms
round the thing — and despite
myself — held my fingers tighter
as it stung.

Kleptomania

Names, Darling, Names
Prada, Miu Miu, Gucci —
one more woman is caught on spot,
her wallet void of money;
she's at her prime, her body too hot,
but she wants to look chic, and her best,
adorn herself, and pass the test.

Names, Darling, Names
I don't recall too many brands —
naked and wrapped in the bedsheet,
I block my ears with my hands,
but my eyes with my wardrobe meet:
I have been told to stay meek,
yet my body yearns to speak.

Before Night Meets Dawn

No luggage, save *The Velveteen Rabbit*,
a gift bought ten years ago at Heffers.
My family tug my sleeves, but I tear
apart the heart-strings, stride past
the customs counter, meet an English woman
at the boarding lounge:
Why coming back to London?
Things have changed.
You are not what you were;
He is not what he was.
I rummage my memories for her name,
while she twists and transforms
into a gremlin — blocking my ears,
I flee onto the plane — the passengers
start to babble in alien tongues and
the face re-appears next to me and
breaks into a mischievous smile:
You've boarded the wrong plane!
Yet I do not panic for long
before the plane explodes
and I fall free, disintegrating into
a fire ball of pent-up passion —

    waking with a sweaty forehead,
hand on the chest, I find myself
in London, my bed facing the window:
outside lights and shadows
float and flicker in a whirlpool,
where shrieks blend with the wind
in a sonata of uncertainty.
Inside, the heater is hissing,
the clock ticking:
I listen: *these are real.*
I grip and pull the quilt,
woolly and soft, over my chest;
I rest my palm on my forehead,
savouring my body warmth in
throbbing anticipation:
I am real.

Bluebird

I must have left the windows open —
waking up in the chill of night
I see a blue shadow

invade the room and
spread its wings across the carpet,
casting shades on the table and

tainting the rims of teacups;
it envelops the computer and
rests on the mousepad.

At once the heaviness is gone,
and the heart,
poised between night and morning,

feels wholesome,
till I feel a flutter at the window
and hear the birds chirping —

I open my eyes to find
the room basking in the sun,
but it was no dream:

at the hooting of the car
I rise, stretch, and expect
a knock on the door.

Present

Kind Man Pious Woman

She throws up
Stuff in the mouth,
Pushes open the door,
Homecoming with bites
Brute and bloody:

'I am no Angel.'
'It's okay, m'dear.'
A Handful of ointment
He rubs her back
Where the wings were.

She glows to the rhythm;
He glows watching her face.
They hear the cries,
Feel the land sinking
And they smile.

Performativity

I must look tired that day,
even in the mood for clothes.
At the mall we met again.

'Don't worry, you'll be fine!'
'Life is tough, you know....

But I'm glad it is —
I'll start working this August!'

I threw her a goodbye and walked away
so that I did not see her mouth drop.

Once upon a time she was really sweet,
and mind games were not my forte.

I stopped at the counter:
my eyes met a sweet baby's —
they sparkled, and I cried 'darling!'

$20

'Really good for us —
things have gotten cheap
these couple of years,'
screamed the housewives
around the stalls,
bubbling and bloated
after lunch gatherings.

'Fine quality. Pretty designs.
Cheapest in town.'
Formerly a storekeeper,
now a stall-owner,
he bent and opened
another box of pyjamas,
fresh from the Mainland.

'Cheaper please!'
'Nah — can't get cheaper.'
Colours dazzling,
mouths mumbling,
notes changing,
suspicious glances
across neighbouring stalls.

I ran my fingers
through the garment,
tracing the hands
it had gone through,
my mind breaking down
the meagre $20
into fabric and labour —

In a mere instant
I entered a room
crowded with yellow faces:
feet twitching on paddles,
their exhausted fingers
pulling fabrics
through sewing machines.

Unplug

Lives here recycle like TV soaps:
familiar scenarios, repeated dialogues, clichéd phrases,
props proper, each step measured,
no unstated movement, nor unscripted line,
an extra gesture, or a slight lift of tone —
Cut!

Unplug
from pirated productions
which mean virtually
every single production —

durians hit
and crack open
things hurl ping-pong
across the floor

rebound tendons
and burning muscles
thumping heart
at someone's presence

wasabi in the nose
raw salmon down the throat
hot liquor scorching the stomach

doodles on the wall
smashed paints on cardboard
spilled beads on marble tiles

drumrolls and white dragon
waterfalls from sky
stars glow and rotate —

unlike Van Gogh's:
housed in museums, downloadable via the net
reproduced everywhere —

I try to catch
an infinitude of colours
shapes and sizes

Cup Noodles

A lovely place
our city is, for sure.
Emigrants flew back
just as sudden as they left,
crying out loud,
'We love Hong Kong —
this is our home.'

Thousands of graduates
appear every summer,
fresh out of school,
and jobless right away.
Some shout with empathy,
'Our leaders, come on!
Reform our education!'

Graduates from abroad —
the luckier bunch —
proclaim with pride:
'Thanks to our parents
we've become smarter people
with well paid jobs.
The future is with us.'

Property agents sigh,
rubbing their feet —
another morning of
near-zero business:
'Long gone, long gone!
The fat chance to go
from rags to riches!'

'Who wants to be
a millionaire?'
Me! Me! Me!
'Let go your pride,
kill, or be killed.'
No way? 'Sorry,
but you are out!'

Watching TV last night
I devoured cup noodles,
expecting them to cause
strange breath this morning —
but I was hungry,
and too lazy to cook
a proper meal.

Screens

'The Gulf War did not take place,'
proclaims Jean Baudrillard —
hence after WTC collapsed
we heard prophecies of Nostradamus
above the cries of suffering
and saw the Devil's face
crystallise in flames.

Large screens are everywhere
in Central, Causeway Bay and
Tsimshatsui, making giants
out of caked celebrities —
we are symbols of youth and health;
we don't smoke, don't take drugs;
we despise casual sex.

Caught in traffic another day,
I caught countless TV screens
at a shop exploding by
the civil servants' march,
before I saw those leaders —
multiplied and holier than life,
reiterating their reiterations.

Disneyland was set up as an illusion
for us visitors to confirm
the reality of the real —
yet didn't Zhuang Zi wonder if
he dreamt of becoming a butterfly
or it was the butterfly indeed
that dreamt of him all along?

Tired of un-caking those faces,
both strange and familiar,
I smashed screen after screen
but found it impossible indeed —
hence I stepped through canvas,
landed on shaking ground and marched
in bold, steady steps.

IOU

Gone are the days
when people cried:
'I don't owe you anything —
Don't bother me!'

Bosses owe their staff
a few months' pay
to rent new flats
that overlook the harbour.

The rich announce bankruptcy
and dismiss their creditors
before they dine as usual
at Fuk Lam Moon.

How have they managed
to overcome insomnia?
Then I doubt if it's ever
plagued them the slightest.

The interview is on air
as I am tending the fire:
'I promise to pay
once we've got the money.'

Cough!
I choke,
stealing a sip
from the veggie soup —

this is just prelude
to steamed fish, soy chicken
and a lot more
I've owed my beloved.

Mother's Choice

Don't the teachers say
here's a good girl gone astray?
Moralists call her a tart
for tearing our society apart.
Church people, all wise and kind,
have to speak God's mind:
Do not murder — hence abortion
is out of the question.
Her friends say, 'Here is one cheapie
who tried to keep men with her body;
I had meant to be subtle
but she's one bad example!'
Even neighbours greet her and stare,
'Where's her man? Where?'
But she's got no man — long turned a monster
She is choked with anger.

Then evening falls —
She hides her fangs and claws.
She stops her roar
as the maid answers the door.
Welcomed by her baby
she unwraps the teddy.
With one hand she cracks an egg,
her other hand massages her leg;
soon the house is steamy with food
and things have never been so good.
After dinner, let's bathe together
till our skins beam with lather;
I'll hum you a new lullaby
so when Maria arrives you won't cry.
Let's keep on praying for a better tomorrow
when the sane will take over the shallow.

MTR

plugged ears in the sea of heads
knees knocking, bodies pressing
sweat dripping, odours mixing
train pulling, the next stop coming

muffled notes pushing the tempo
on the crest of human waves
a trumpet rising, a tango forming
keep pulling, keep flowing

Love in the time of SARS

6pm. Colleagues gathered
and blocked the TV —
heads still, breath held —
waited for the latest figure,
prayed for fewer cases.

She avoided the lift
and went down the stairs —
shadows floated past —
some ninety-nine steps,
or more? She lost count.

Eyes teary and red.
Eyes flooded the KCR ride.
Eyes staring into eyes —
Eyes drooping, gazes averted —
Eyes full of doubts? Or fear?

She checked her mobile —
no missing calls —
she'd missed his voice.
Her fingers were itchy,
her throat, phlegm-choked.

7pm. At her home PC —
his email just arrived —
she smiled, mask-free.
Hunger struck her:
she remembered her dinner.

Do I Dare?

Our home, our sweet home, should now burst with cheers:
It's six o'clock, the moment of the day —
Mama's on the sofa, huddled in tears.
She leans on Papa, and her head's turned grey.

He chided me, as his way of loving me.
Oh no, I never saw him cry before:
The lines between his brows deepen, and he
Starts sobbing, choking, till his face goes sore.

And where is Sis? She's with her choir at school:
Her eyes get blurry till they miss a key;
Her students, shocked and sad, still keep their cool
As her fingers search for the middle C.

If that ever happened, no one would care:
The night roars on, dancers rave, billboards beam.
Such thoughts do arise, like in a bad dream —
And I saw them: Do I dare? Do I dare?

Birthday Present

In a window seat
I finished my Häagen-Dazs
as my glance wanders
from the magazine
to the October street
coloured and festivied
by winter displays.

'*Now is a gift, and
that's why it is called present,*'
someone emailed me,
leaving out the banal bit:
Each day is a new beginning —

On my way to work
after a half-day break
the autumnal tunes
gather in me a profound
déjà vu, déjà senti —
which I try to un-feel
to feel again.

About the Author

AMY LAI was born in Hong Kong, received her education in Hong Kong and England, and now lectures in Literature and Cultural Studies at the Hong Kong University of Science and Technology. *Present* is her first poetry book.

Printed in the United States
36329LVS00001B/183